SB

Whanki Museum
Kyu Sung Woo

Edited by Oscar Riera Ojeda
Introduction by Hong-bin Kang

Rockport Publishers
Gloucester, Massachusetts

SINGLE BUILDING Series | Process of an Architectural Work

First published in the
United States of America by:
Rockport Publishers, Inc.
33 Commercial Street
Gloucester, Massachusetts 01930-5089
Telephone: (978) 282-9590
Facsimile: (978) 283-2742

Distributed to the book trade
and art trade in the United States by:
North Light Books, an imprint of
F & W Publications
1507 Dana Avenue
Cincinnati, Ohio 45207
Telephone: (800) 289-0963

Other Distribution by:
Rockport Publishers, Inc.
Gloucester, Massachusetts 01930-5089

ISBN 1-56496-524-4

10 9 8 7 6 5 4 3 2 1

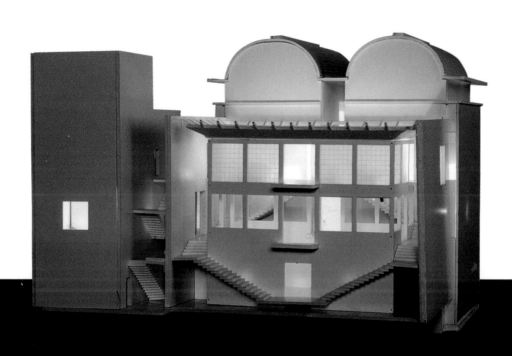

contents

by Hong-bin Kang

The Whanki Museum, built in 1992, commemorates and houses the works of Kim Whanki, a painter and pioneer of modern art

in Korea. With its combination of lyricism and logic, its evocation of nature and its meticulous construction of order, the muse-

um gracefully embodies the spirit of the painter. At the same time, it is emblematic of the design philosophy of its architect,

Kyu Sung Woo. ∎ Woo, a Korean-born architect working in the United States, grew up in Seoul and Kaesung (now part of

North Korea) during the turbulent period of Korean history that followed the end of the Korean War. After graduating from

Seoul National University with a degree in architecture in 1963, he worked at the Institute of Housing, Urban and Regional

Planning under the Korean Ministry of Construction. There, Woo met American architect Oswald Nagler, who trained him in

urban design and later encouraged him to continue his studies in the United States. ∎ Woo came to the United States to

study at Columbia University in 1967. At Columbia, he was particularly influenced by the philosophy of Victor Christ-Janer,

who emphasized the importance of a substructural or "primal imagery." It was also during this time that Woo met artist Kim

Whanki. Woo continued his architectural studies at the Harvard Graduate School of Design, where he met Jose Luis Sert. Upon

graduation he entered Sert's architectural office. ∎ During the five-year period in which he worked closely with Sert, Woo

gained an education in design that would greatly inform his later techniques and practices. With Sert as a mentor, he worked

on both American and European projects. His own cross-cultural efforts would later parallel those of Sert, who was similarly

a foreign-born architect practicing in the United States. Woo's work on the expansion of Fondation Maeght Museum in 1973

Fondation Maeght exterior view, Jose Luis Sert 1964
(upper right) Ho Am Art Museum section model (above)
Arts of Korea gallery at the Metropolitan Museum of Art,
Kyu Sung Woo Architect 1998 (lower right)

was also his first experience in museum design. ▌ Woo left Sert's office to develop his own design ideas in 1974, first working

as senior urban designer for the City of New York. Then, in 1978, he began his own practice in Cambridge while teaching

design studios at the Massachusetts Institute of Technology's department of architecture and the Harvard Graduate School of

Design. ▌ Woo's work has included museums, housing and urban design, and private homes. Arts-related projects include

design of the new Korean gallery at the Metropolitan Museum of Art (1998), exhibit design for a show on Chinese Furniture

at the Peabody Museum in Salem, Massachusetts (1996) and the Hoam Art Museum Complex (unbuilt) in Yongin, Korea.

Housing and urban design projects include the Athletes' and Reporters' Village for the 24th Olympiad in Seoul (1988),

Observatory Hill Commons Faculty Housing at Harvard University (1990), and Wheeler Hill in Columbia, South Carolina (1979).

Public projects include the Jordan Pond House in Acadia National Park, Maine (1982), and Fort Adams Daycare in Newport,

Rhode Island (1985). Private residences include "Stonecloud" in Seoul, Korea (1997), the Woo House in Cambridge,

Massachusetts (1989), and artist Kim Tschang-yeul's residence in Seoul, Korea (1988). ▌ Woo has designed buildings in both

Korea and the United States. In a sense it is meaningless to ask if Woo is a "Korean" architect or an "American" architect: for

he is neither, and at the same time, both. As one critic remarked, Woo appears to maintain "a critical distance" from both Korea

and the United States. He does not try to sell "Oriental" qualities to the American architectural community, nor does he

attempt to introduce the latest in Western architecture to Koreans. ▌ Woo avoids talking about his work, and does not actively

"Stonecloud" entry steps, entry court and steps to roof terrace

participate in the discussions on architectural theory that fill the pages of architectural journals. He thinks about architecture by asking questions, questions whose answers lie in the queries themselves. How will the whole of a building relate to the parts? How will each element relate to the others? For Woo, design is not a process of creating something out of nothing, and he refuses to fix forms and images in advance. Rather, he allows his design to evolve from specific circumstance, and considers it his particular mission to create places where the experience of architecture itself speaks a solution to formal questions. ∎ While one will find that Woo eschews purely conceptual solutions in his design, one can also detect a consistent "color" in his work that is rooted in the strength of his concept of architecture. The phrase "aesthetic of restraint" defines this color. There are no dazzling visual effects or provocative configurations in Woo's buildings: exaggeration, recklessness, and highhandedness are absent from his work. Instead, a quiet inner order pervades his buildings, an order that seeps calmly and unconsciously into the observer's mind. The appeal of Woo's architecture lies in his elegant blending of logic and lyricism, and the building that best demonstrates this allure is the Whanki Museum.   ∎ A Duet of Architecture and Art The designer of a museum, especially one that commemorates a specific artist, is faced with two conflicting demands. On the one hand, the building must recede into the background so that the art on exhibit takes center stage. On the other hand, it must manifest itself in a structure commemorating the work and life of the artist. ∎ Like Whanki's paintings, Woo's Whanki Museum is a quiet yet self-assured jewel. Though the product of lucid thought, it touches and moves the heart. It does not draw attention to itself with exaggerated features, yet it is filled with inner energy. It is modest yet penetrating, and manages to project a certain richness while employing a language of great restraint. Through this museum, Woo fully illustrates his unique logic and poetic imagination. ▌ The Whanki Museum is hidden in a ravine in a residential area not far from the president's mansion in Seoul. Located on a scenic site facing Mount In Wang San to the west and Mount Puk Ak San to the south, it is deliberately removed from the gallery district in the heart of the capital. Woo helped select the site, which retains the feeling of the Seoul that predates the city's present manifestation as a commercial metropolis, the "old Seoul" where both artist and architect spent their youth. ▌ Woo created a complex structure for the Whanki Museum, where several buildings, some detached and others connected, form the larger whole. The function of the museum and the topographical conditions achieve an ingenious harmony in this composition. The layout permits the staging of various functions, such as permanent and special exhibitions, meetings and seminars, and provides a humane and intimate environment despite the relatively large building area on a sloped site. The museum structure and the overall atmosphere, including the buildings and courtyard, draw visitors into an integrated space that commemorates Kim and provides an arena for intense personal experience. ▌ The main building is composed of three "building groups." Curatorial functions are held in a stack of square modules on axis with the entrance. A rectangular building crowned with a pair of vaults is the exhibition hall, while the cubic space between these two buildings is the central hall. These three building groups are linked by stairs that spiral upward around them. It is interesting to

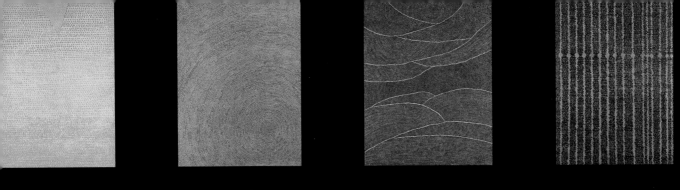

Untitled works by Kim Whanki. Left to right: 14-12-71, oil on cotton, 292x210cm; 14-03-71, oil on cotton, 250x193cm; 16-09-73, oil on cotton, 264x208.2cm; 22-10-73, oil on cotton, 180x130cm

note the 3:2:1 relationship of these building groups. The curatorial building is created by three overlapping hexahedrons, the exhibition hall is composed of two vaults, and the central hall is situated inside a single hexahedron. This relationship imparts an order of primitive and intense contrast and unity to the main building. ▮ A tour of the Museum begins at the entrance hall, a tall, narrow space flooded with light from above, aligned on axis with the entrance of the curatorial building. A large black-and-white paneled likeness of the painter at work greets visitors. High on the side wall, a section of a line drawing by Kim Whanki has been transformed into stained glass. Light filters through it from the south, projecting its image into the entrance hall. ▮ Past the entrance hall and across a small transitional space is the central hall. An eight-meter cube, the hall is the nucleus of the Whanki Museum, and its presence is felt throughout the complex. Here, the duet between architect and painter is most strikingly realized. The white of the lower walls envelop Kim Whanki's paintings and highlight them so that they are set as brilliant jewels. Above the paintings, the walls seem to disappear, while above the walls, columns and stairs lead the eye to the highest level of the building and up to the sky. Enclosed and open spaces, planes and lines, light and shadow—a subtle drama of contrast and unity unfolds within the orderly geometric framework, transforming the central hall into a sanctuary dedicated to the art of Kim Whanki, a monument created out of empty space. ▮ Spiraling stairs, which wrap around the back of the four walls demarcating the central hall, lead visitors to the exhibition hall. Light pouring in from a skylight creates the feeling that one is outside; as a result, one experiences the empty space of the central hall as an independent structure with

Object (paper mache), 9.5x9.5in Kim Whanki 1968 (left)
Object (paper maché), 32.5x20x20cm Kim Whanki 1968
(right) Object (paper maché), Kim Whanki 1968 (below right)

its own physical entity. The designer clearly wanted to bestow a certain monumentality upon the central hall. The transitional

space created between the stairs and the exhibition space continues the theme of formal articulation which enables one to

perceive spaces as both separate and interconnected. ▌ Exhibition space on the second and third floors consists of two cozy

areas intended for separate exhibitions. Nowhere does one feel that the architectural device competes with the paintings:

rather, an effective background is cautiously and meticulously created by the design of the museum. When a wall meets a wall,

or a wall a ceiling, they cross paths rather than collide, so that walls and ceilings become less demarcations of internal space

than the supporting framework for the art they contain. ▌ Where there are decided points of juncture in the building,

exchange with the world outside the exhibition hall takes place. Sunlight seeps through a hidden skylight, and the majestic

shape of Mt. In Wang San is framed in a vertical window. As a result of this presentation, the exhibition hall comes alive as

a space in which nature's breath can be felt. The air and light flow as in one of Whanki's paintings. The exhibition hall is not

simply an enclosed warehouse. Through restraint and modesty, the museum's designer has succeeded in making the entire

exhibition space a stirring landscape of mental images. ▌ A square courtyard outside the exhibition hall, located on the roof

of the central hall, is enclosed on all four sides like the central garden of a traditional Korean house. A long corridor of glass

blocks with a tin roof surrounds the courtyard, turning it into a space that faces the sky. At the center of the courtyard is a

well-like skylight that sends light into the central hall below. The silhouettes of the two round vaults in the exhibition hall stand proudly beyond the western corridor. ▍ The courtyard ambiance, generated through a combination of squares and circles,

glass and metal, is abstract and tempered. It stands in sharp contrast to the surrounding natural environment, Whanki's paintings,

and the lyrical space of the museum's interior. This contrast is clearly intentional. It brings visitors closer to the trees and rocks,

the mountains and valleys, the wind and clouds visible through openings in the gallery. Through geometrical abstraction,

Woo asks the visitor to ruminate on the museum's theme, "the manifestation of nature and the universe through a landscape

of mental images." ▍ From the outside, the Main Building appears simple and serene. Indeed, it is difficult to imagine the

diverse, dynamic drama taking place inside the simple cubic structure overlaid with slabs of stone. One can sense an extraor-

dinary refinement in details, such as the copper lining between the stone slabs at the corner of the building, the different quality

of the stone slabs themselves, and the vaults on the roof. Yet there is no trace of formal decoration or an attempt to impress

visitors with visual effects. Still, there is a lofty pride evident in the Whanki Museum. It comes not only from the buildings

themselves, but from the way they are arranged. Just as the stairs inside the building accentuate the central hall by circling

its outer walls, the paved space on the roof and the stairs encircling the Main Building enable the museum to adhere closely

to the site's sloped topography, asserting a consistent and monumental independence. ▍ The Whanki Museum represents the

quintessence of Woo's architecture. There are no loud messages or gestures in this structure, nor are there any façades or

skylines produced for the camera's benefit. The Whanki Museum is not a structure of visual completion, but a place of consummate personal experience. The museum reveals its true form only when one experiences its interior and exterior, the paintings on display, and the background as one. ∎

Hong-bin Kang ∎ Seoul, Korea ∎ December 1, 1997

Hong-bin Kang was born in Seoul, Korea in 1945. He received a Ph.D. in arts, architecture and environmental studies from the Massachusetts Institute of Technology. He also holds a master of architecture degree in urban design from the Graduate School of Design at Harvard University. He is presently a professor at the University of Seoul department of urban planning. Among his numerous positions he served as director general in policy and planning of the Seoul Metropolitan Government from 1990 to 1996; director of the Housing Research Institute of the Korea National Housing Corporation from 1985 to 1990 and director of urban design of the Environmental Planning Institute of the Seoul National University Graduate School of Environmental Studies from 1981 to 1985.

Early in 1988, the Whanki Foundation decided to build a museum for the works of painter Kim Whanki in Seoul, Korea. Whanki had lived in New York and Paris, and these cities were also considered as possible locations, but Seoul was ultimately chosen so that the artist's works could be kept as a collection in Korea. Buam Dong Valley was chosen over other sites in and around the city because of its central location, strong character, and emotive power. ∎ In August of 1988, after the site had been selected, Mrs. Hyangan Kim, wife of the deceased painter, requested that I design the museum. I had been close to Kim Whanki, and as I designed I reflected at length on his life and work. I wanted to create a space for his works that would complement the elements of nature that were so important to his art—the moon, mountains, clouds, rocks and trees. At the same time, I wanted the space to have a modern sensibility. ∎ Because of my association with Mrs. Kim and the Foundation, I had been involved in the planning of the museum from its earliest stages, which included site selection, program development and project management. During the design period, I worked with Mrs. Kim and Dominique Bozo, then President of the Pompidou Center in Paris. I found Mr. Bozo's input particularly helpful in refining the circulation scheme; defining the program; and articulating the relationships between the museum, the city, and the landscape. Mr. Bozo visited the site in August 1992, when construction was still underway, but passed away the following spring before the museum was complete. ∎ When I first began designing the museum, the site designated for the project was limited to the area around the current main building, and the program consisted of permanent exhibits, temporary exhibitions and other support spaces such as

From left to right, Mrs. Hyangan Kim, Whanki Museum Director Kwang-Su Oh, Kyu Sung Woo and Pompidou Center President (at that time) Dominique Bozo, during a construction site visit (above) Kim Whanki in his New York City Studio 1971 (right)

a library, cafe, shop and lobby. During the construction of the main building, which began in September 1991, the foundation acquired additional property for the construction of a building for temporary exhibitions and lectures, a parking area, and a garden. The additional property extended the building site to the west, and improved its composition by giving the relatively high main building a spacious entry. ∎ Overall, the design period was proportionately much greater than the construction period, due to a lengthy approval process with the city, which delayed construction. The long design period was beneficial in many ways, but the shortened construction period that followed made the task of completing the museum a difficult one. The main building was finally completed in1992, while the annex building and landscape were completed in November of 1993.

∎ **Buam Dong Valley** Buam Dong, the very narrow valley where the museum is located, runs east-to-west at the foothills of Buk Han San mountain. High on the eastern side of the mountain, the old city wall Buk Han San Sung is visible, while on the west, down across the valley, the remarkable rock formations of In Wang San come to view. Buam Dong is one of several valleys that define most of the historic neighborhoods in Seoul. Like the other valley neighborhoods of the city, the Buam Dong Valley encompasses its own distinctive visual field. Also like many of Seoul's other residential communities, the valley that accommodates the Whanki Museum is rapidly changing, due to new economic and social conditions. One- and two-story houses surround the museum site, and many two- and three-story multi-family housing complexes are being constructed. Meanwhile, the current street networks are not entirely organized, and relationships between the buildings are governed only by the limits set by property bounds. As I designed the Whanki Museum, I tried to consider how to conform the museum's existence as a public building to the scale of its neighborhood, its topography, and its natural environment. ▮ **The Museum** Unlike painting and sculpture, architecture has a program. The program of a museum is to provide a suitable environment for the exhibition and preservation of artwork, create a place for education and assembly, and generate a contemplative space for contemporary society. At the same time, a museum presents an architectural experience. Often, conflict between the purpose of a museum and the character of its architecture becomes a matter of controversy. The issue of whether an exhibition space provides proper conditions in which to view and appreciate art often leads to questions of whether an appreciation of the artwork will be disturbed by imposed architectural conditions. Once the basic conditions of exhibition are satisfied, the relationship between the artwork that is to be exhibited and the space that exhibits can vary greatly. In the case of temporary exhibitions, space is designed based on common characteristics of artwork that might be exhibited. In other cases, exhibit space can be designed for a specific work of art, or art can be designed specifically for an existing or preconceived space. Because most of the space in the Whanki Museum was intended for the permanent collection of a single artist's work, the character of the museum and the gallery design were determined largely by known variables, and could be more specific than those of a museum whose primary function might be to host works by diverse artists. Still, because of the variety in Whanki's works, and because exhibits in the museum would occasionally change, I aimed to create a museum that would be flexible in

Site view from the south, before construction

23

accommodating a range of artwork. I was careful in planning the size of the walls, lighting scheme, materials, and other aspects of the museum that would help to determine the character of the exhibition spaces. ▌ In exhibition spaces, the architectural experience should be subordinate to that of the art. Here and elsewhere, however, architecture does not have to play a passive role. The process of absorbing art is a collective and continuous experience that occurs throughout a museum, an intense activity that needs intervals of rest. Occasional connections with nature and the context, activated by the architecture of a museum, can enhance one's experience of a work of art and make one's appreciation of it both more relevant and rich. Thus it is important to introduce natural light into a museum and to provide ways for people in the building to recognize and be aware of the nature that exists outside. In the end, the experience of architecture and the appreciation of artwork are both necessary components of the museum experience. Rather than conflict, these components can complement each other to make the entire experience of a museum more profound.   ▌ **Architecture** Buam Dong Valley's small scale could not accommodate a bulky building. The limited area and complex shape of the site, combined with the requirement for high ceilings in exhibit and common spaces, forms a volume that is large for the surrounding residential area. For the massing to accommodate these difficult conditions, a significant portion of the program is located underground and the remaining building is fragmented into several pieces to form a small village. Each building in the composition has its own form, function and meaning. Together, they form a whole which is the museum. This additive method to site planning, which follows the topography, has been

commonly used in Korean architecture. Korean palaces and temples often address similar small-scale topography. The museum

buildings, grouped around a central courtyard within the walled compound, follow the axis of the valley. Along this axis, higher

northern buildings coincide with and mediate between northern slopes of the mountain and the southern buildings of the

site. The orientation of the southern building aligns with the edge of the property, providing a secondary axis in the main

building complex. The siting and organization of the annex building near the entrance acknowledges both directions. These

relationships among the building components reflect the small and large order within the valley. ▌ The coinciding directions

between the building and the valley not only emphasize the spatial flow of the valley, but help to form spaces between the

buildings. This relationship enhances the eastern view of the city wall and the rock formations in the distance. Similarly, a

series of walls running east-to-west cuts the chaotic view across the narrow valley. Following the land, the buildings recreate

the changing ground plane. The upper galleries roofed by two barrel vaults give significant volume and meaning to the

permanent collection pavilion. The stepping building rises floor by floor on the southeastern boundary, corresponding to

the scale of the surrounding small houses and suggesting the adjoining steep hillside. The entire building is organized by

a series of uniquely defined edges to a collective center marked by light. This produces an inwardly focused composition that

is adjusted to receive light and acknowledge the external conditions of the site. ▌ Building materials for the museum are used

as in traditional Korean architecture. The intersection of building and ground is stone treated as masonry. Above, the stone is

Chang Duk Palace, Seoul, Korea, site plan (far left) Traditional
Korean architecture-wall (left) Bul Kook Sa (temple), Kyung Ju,
Korea (right) Traditional Korean rare garden (bottom)

expressed as a plane and rises to the lead-coated copper roof. The rough-textured retaining stone is Moon Kyung Suk and the

wall surfaces that are inserted with lead coated copper are Po Chun Suk treated as a stone sheet. The annex building's exte-

rior is cement brick, the same as the compound walls, to express its ordinary nature and contrast with the special character of

the main building. Materials are used to reinforce meanings established by the massing and program, as well as to recognize their

own material properties. ▌ The interior space of the museum is formed around an eight-meter cubic underground space,

located below the exterior courtyard. This space accommodates exhibitions and assembly functions as well as other activities.

It is the museum's center of circulation and orientation. Each exhibition space is connected by staircases that surround this

plaza. The exterior walls of these staircases are washed by daylight to relieve the confined feeling of being underground as

well as to suggest the exterior world. At the center of the complex and at the beginning of the staircases to the east lies a

deep, dark pond of water that enhances a primal image of light, water and containment underground. ▌ While complex in

their conception, the spaces of the museum are simple in execution. They develop their richness through a variety of light,

subtle materials and interconnected movement. Between the exhibition spaces and central court are connecting zones which

reinforce the meaning of the major spaces and provide the necessary area for secondary movement, storage and mechanical

services. The movement systems are organized in a series of intersecting routes that give the visitor a choice of experiences.

The pattern of circulation is not as efficient as a linear system, but in the case of exhibition, since the purpose of space is movement, the alternative routes add to the experience and lessen the severity of level differences within the site. ▌ Most of the interior spaces are painted white. Walls and ceilings are treated with the same material and color, thus limiting the plastic character to size and form only. Artificial lighting is used in exhibition spaces for controlled illumination of the artwork. This control gives the ability to conserve light-sensitive works. Except for drawings, all exhibition spaces have daylight introduced to enhance the sense of space and connection to the outside. The two exhibition spaces on the second floor are given indirect daylight through clerestory openings at the upper portion of the third floor. For the upper-level exhibition spaces, light reflects between the two vaults and washes the ceilings. This lighting effect changes its property according to the time of day and direction of the sun. It reflects various colors of light—cold and warm, blue and red—giving different renderings to the walls and ceilings. ▌ Because the museum is located in a major city, the exterior space is designed to provide the maximum area for rest, to enrich the experience of the museum. All of the spaces within the compound walls, except the steep northern slope, are planned to provide landscaped walks or other contemplative areas. Between the gate and the main building is a major outdoor space with two prominent pine trees. These trees mark the entry court for the main building and the annex. Behind the courtyard of the central building, a walkway punctuated with steps connects to a small garden of stepping walls with flowers. These exterior spaces are again organized by an intersecting system of movement that occasionally interfaces with the interior circulation to provide a variety of interior and exterior spatial experiences. ▌ In the end, a museum is a public institution that transcends the process of its construction. People who use a museum change through time, but the artwork it houses lives on, and the museum remains. Thus I tried to base the design of the Whanki Museum on lasting issues, knowing that the building would inevitably be of our own time. These issues included the building's relationship to the topography and properties of the land, and the order of the building's spatial structure as an intrinsic whole. I would like to think that the building will become both new and familiar as time passes.

Kyu Sung Woo ▐ Cambridge, Massachusetts ▐ December 15, 1997

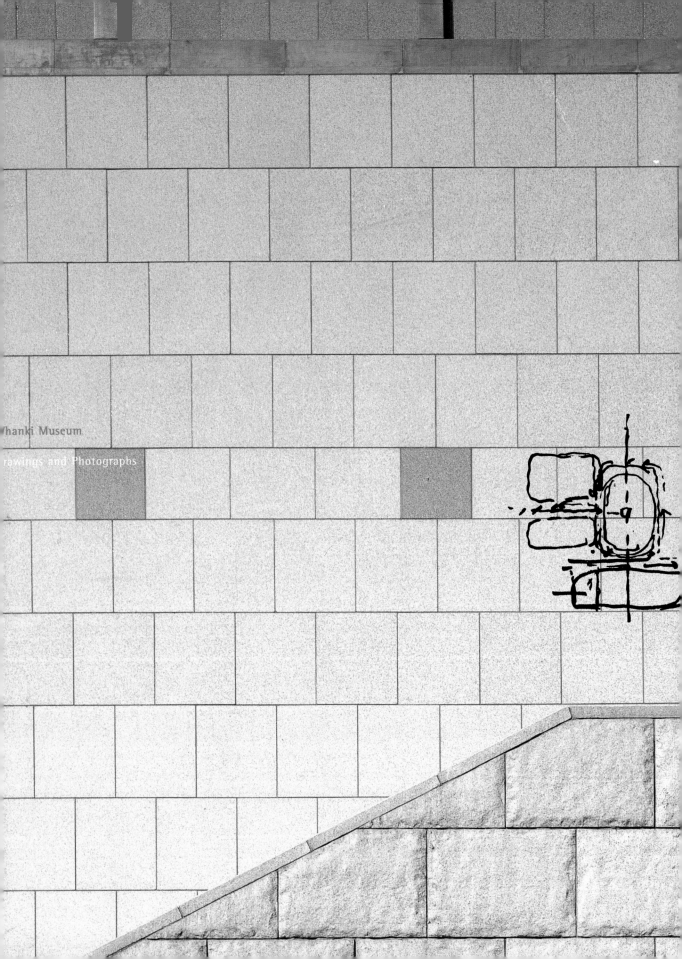

Whanki Museum

rawings and Photographs

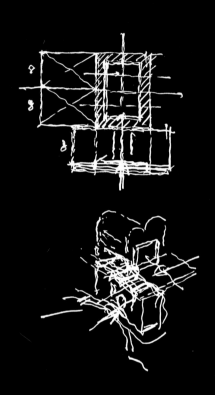

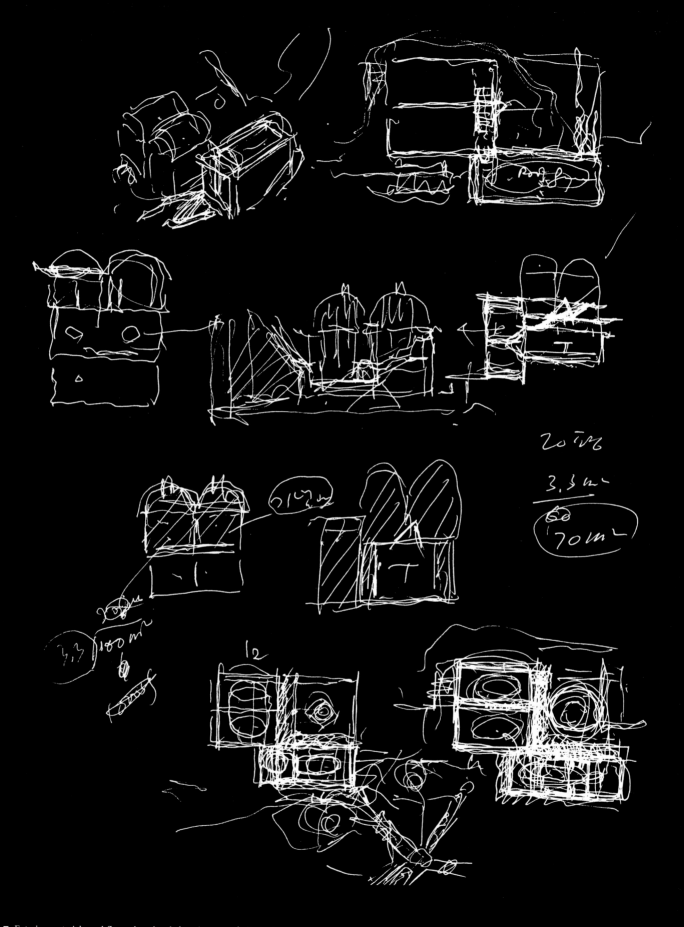

7 Exterior materials and floor plan sketch (previous page) Early floor plans and volumatric sketches (this spread) Axonometric of interior circulation (foldout page)

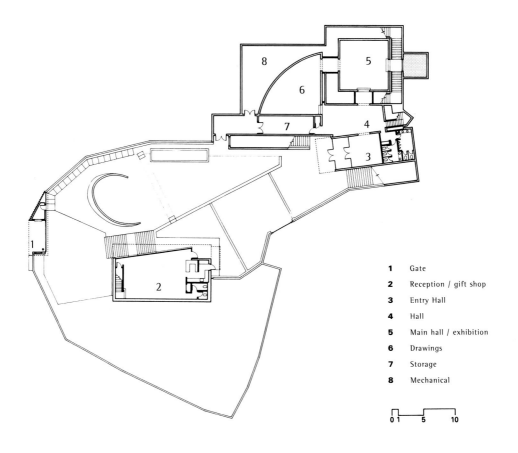

1   Gate
2   Reception / gift shop
3   Entry Hall
4   Hall
5   Main hall / exhibition
6   Drawings
7   Storage
8   Mechanical

0 1   5   10

First floor plan (above)   Section looking east (below)

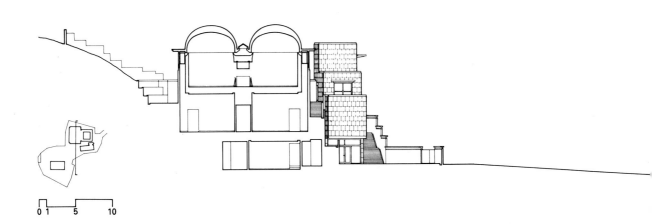

0 1   5   10

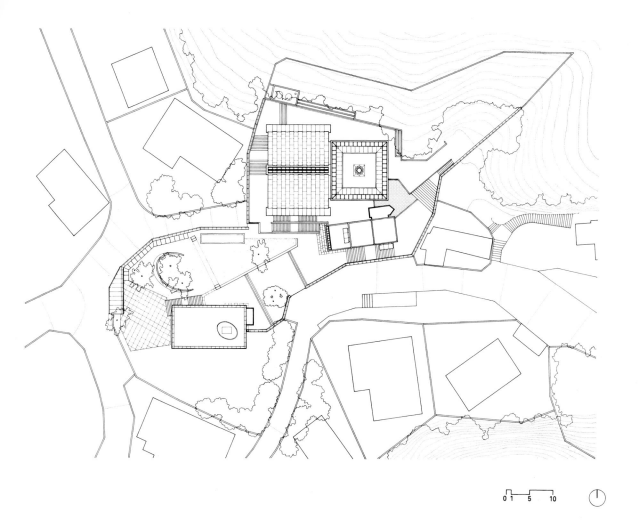

Site plan (above) Section looking east (below)

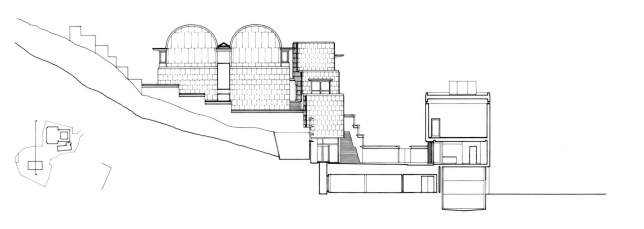

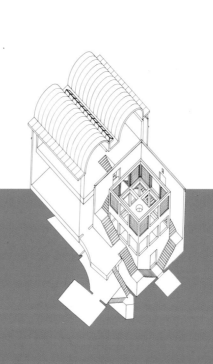

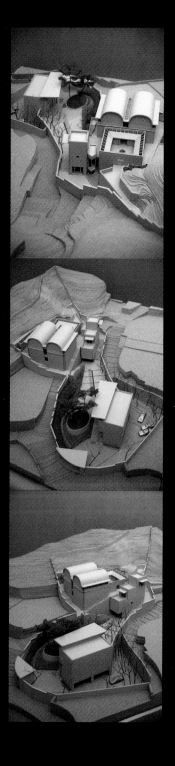

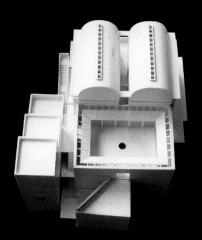

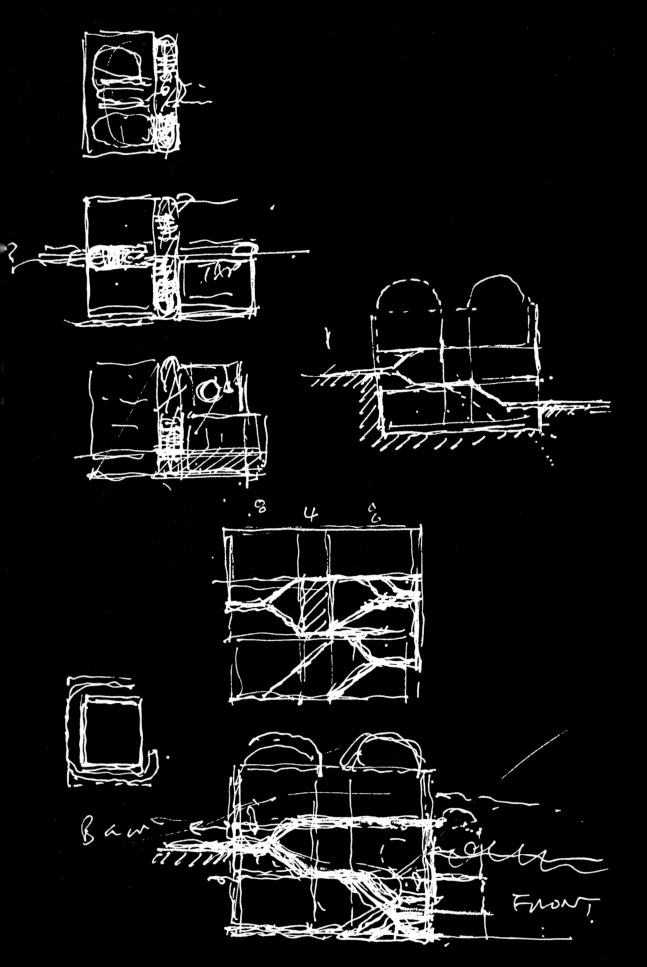

Early floor plans and volumetric sketches (this page) Axonometric (previous foldout page)

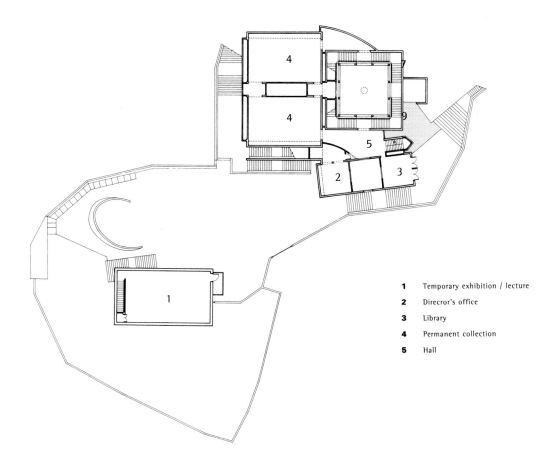

1   Temporary exhibition / lecture

2   Direcror's office

3   Library

4   Permanent collection

5   Hall

Second floor plan (above) Section looking north (below)

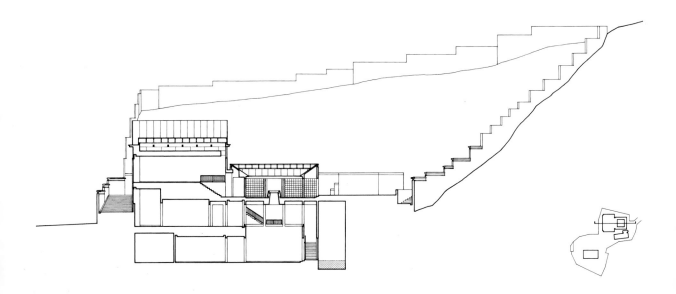

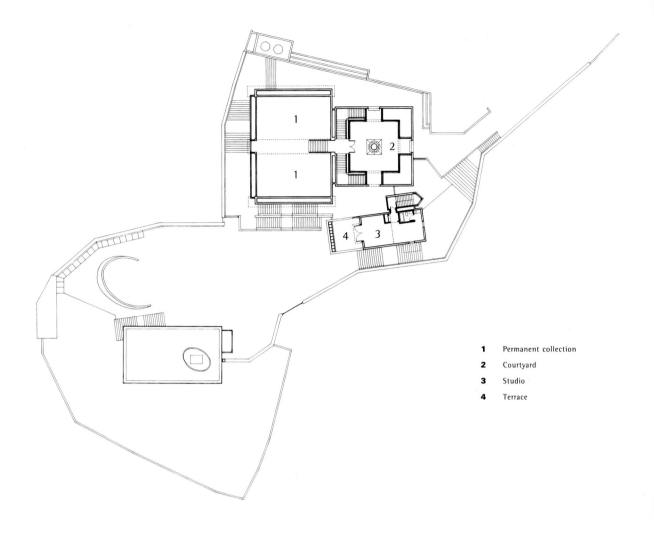

1   Permanent collection

2   Courtyard

3   Studio

4   Terrace

Third floor plan (above) Section looking west (below)

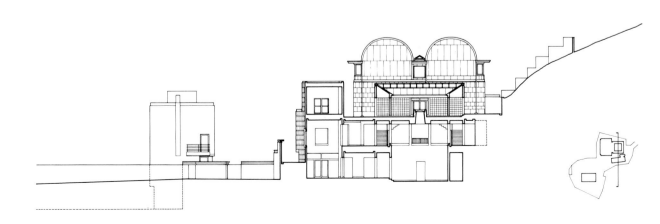

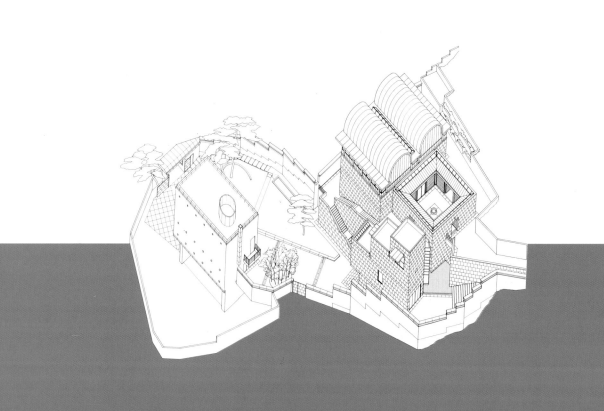

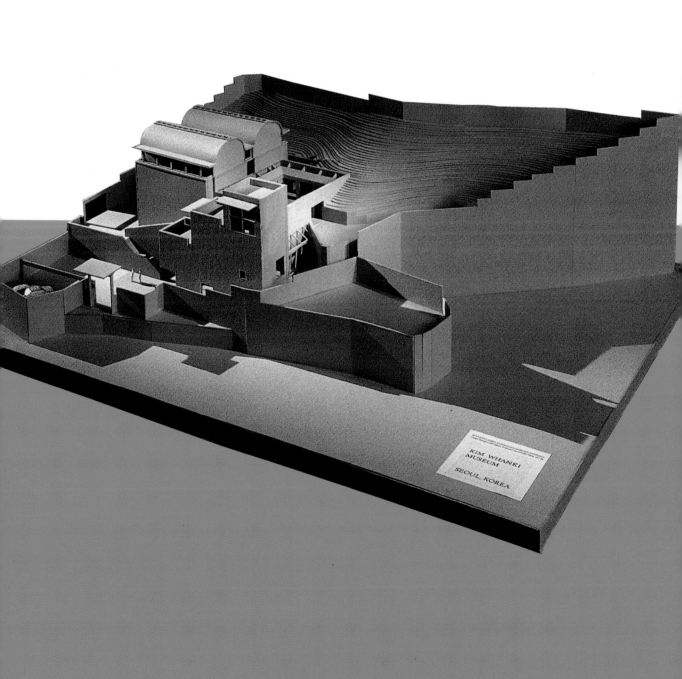

KIM WHANKI
MUSEUM

SEOUL KOREA

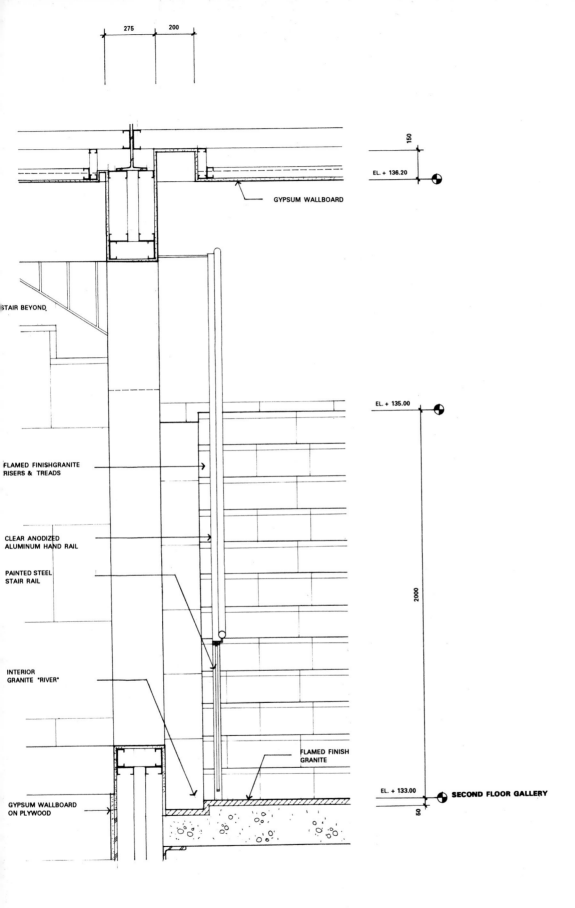

275   200

150

EL. + 136.20

GYPSUM WALLBOARD

STAIR BEYOND

EL. + 135.00

FLAMED FINISHGRANITE
RISERS & TREADS

CLEAR ANODIZED
ALUMINUM HAND RAIL

PAINTED STEEL
STAIR RAIL

2000

INTERIOR
GRANITE "RIVER"

FLAMED FINISH
GRANITE

GYPSUM WALLBOARD
ON PLYWOOD

EL. + 133.00   SECOND FLOOR GALLERY

50

Section through Central Hall wall detail (above) Construction process (this, previous and following spreads)

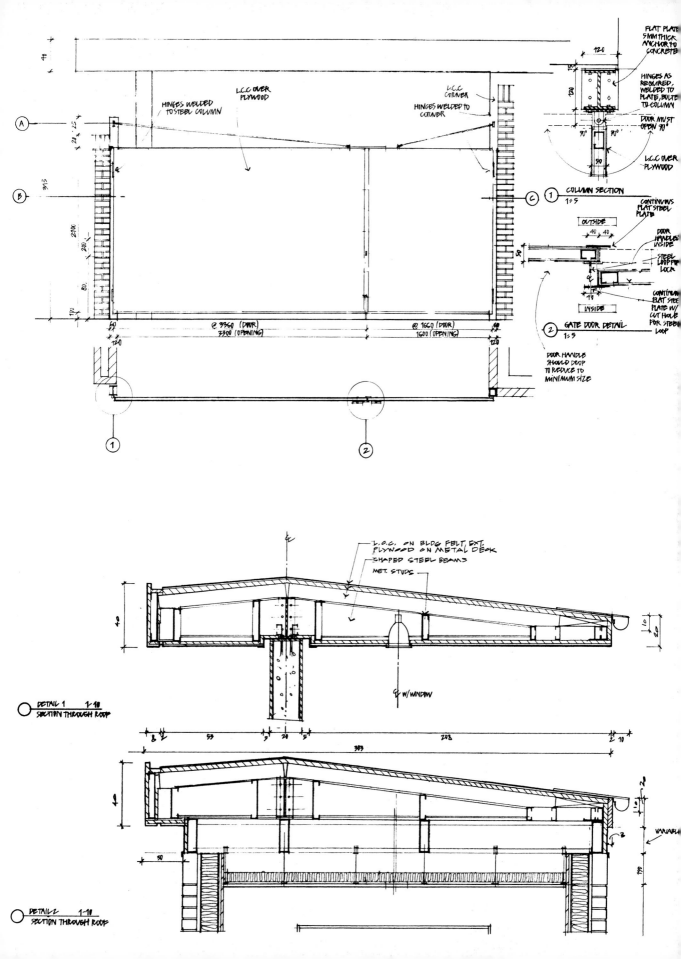

LCC OVER PLYWOOD

LCC CORNER

HINGES WELDED TO STEEL COLUMN

HINGES WELDED TO CORNER

FLAT PLATE 5MM THICK ANCHOR TO CONCRETE

HINGES AS REQUIRED, WELDED TO PLATE, BOLTED TO COLUMN

DOOR MUST OPEN 90°

LCC OVER PLYWOOD

120

90° 90°

50

COLUMN SECTION 1:5

CONTINUOUS FLAT STEEL PLATE

DOOR HANDLES INSIDE

STEEL LOOP FOR LOCK

CONTINUOUS FLAT STEEL PLATE W/ CUT HOLE FOR STEEL LOOP

OUTSIDE

40 40

INSIDE

GATE DOOR DETAIL 1:5

DOOR HANDLE SHOULD DROP TO REDUCE TO MINIMUM SIZE

A

B

C

1

2100

200

50

170

@ 3360 (DOOR)
3300 (OPENING)

@ 1660 (DOOR)
1600 (OPENING)

120

120

1

2

L.O.C. ON BLDG FELT, EXT. PLYWOOD ON METAL DECK

SHAPED STEEL BEAMS

MET. STUDS

W/ WINDOW

DETAIL 1   1:10
SECTION THROUGH ROOF

DETAIL 2   1:10
SECTION THROUGH ROOF

50

VARIABLE

15 16 17 Annex building (previous spread) Temporary exhibition space in Annex building (left) Café and shop at Annex building (above)

WHANKI · NEW YORK · 1963~1974
WHANKI FOUNDATION · YOUNG A
1993.11.5~12.5

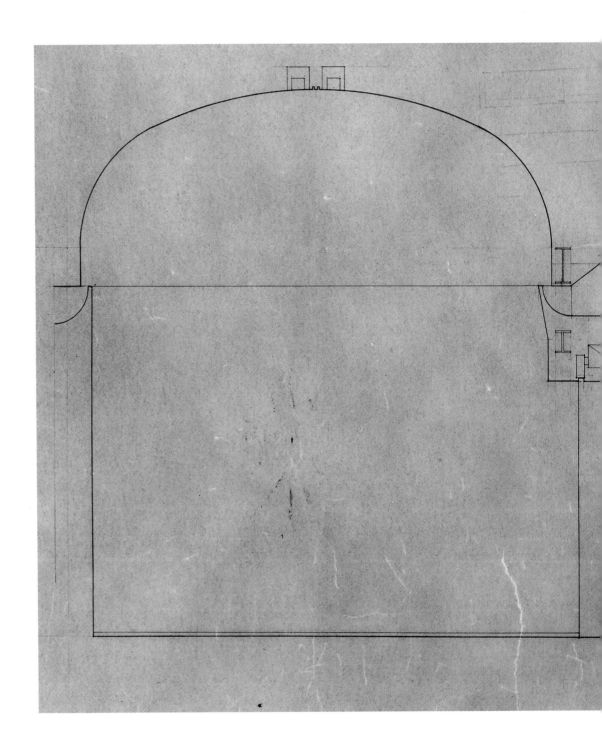

Elevation and section of gallery spaces (left) Section study (above) Axonometric detail of exterior corner (right)

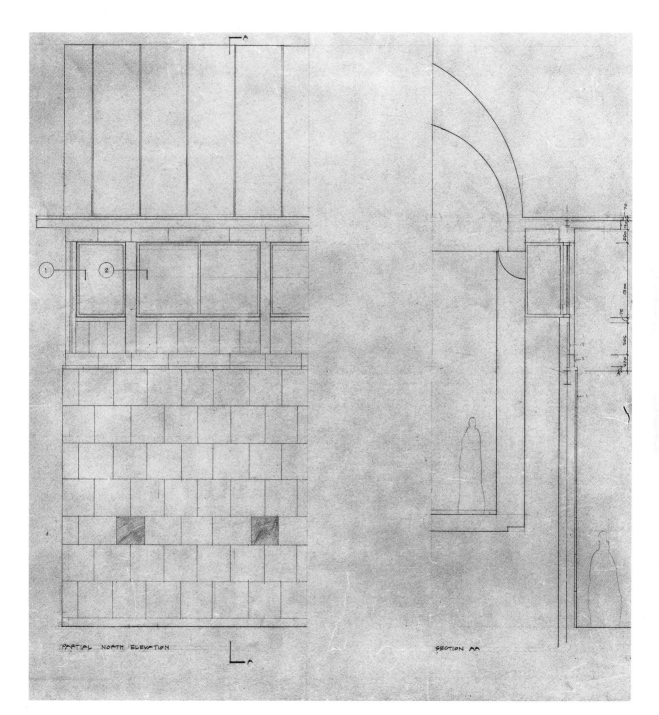

PARTIAL NORTH ELEVATION

SECTION AA

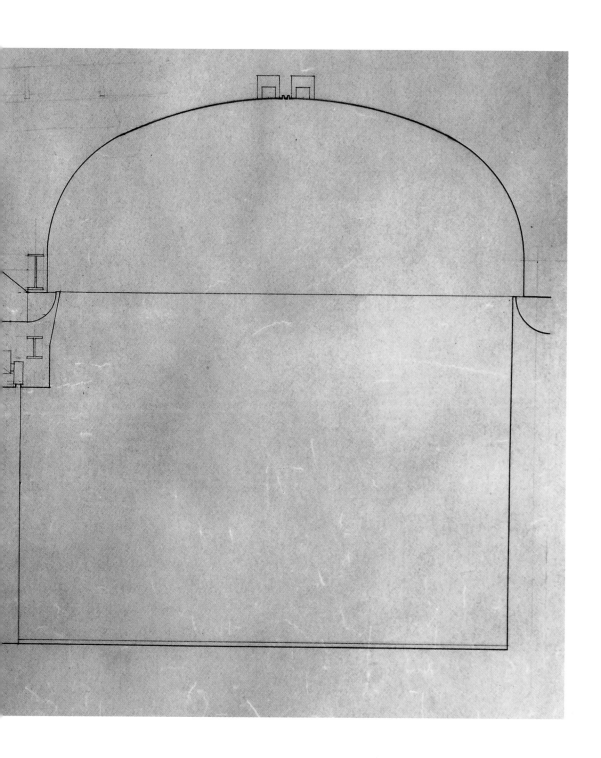

27 28 29 30 Administrative wing (left) Secondary stair and reflecting pool (top) Secondary stair (middle) Reflecting pool area (bottom)

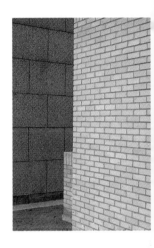

31 32 33 34 35 36 37 East side exterior stair (opposite page) Exterior stair detail (top left) Exterior stair (top center) Terrace (top right) Perimeter wall (middle left) Exterior walls (middle right) Secondary stair exterior detail (bottom)

38 39 Steps at east of site (above) Passage at north of site (opposite page)

40 41 42 43 44 45 Perimeter wall cap (far left); Exterior materials (second from left); Exterior materials detail (middle); Exterior corner detail (second from right); Parapet detail (far right); Exterior stair detail (below)

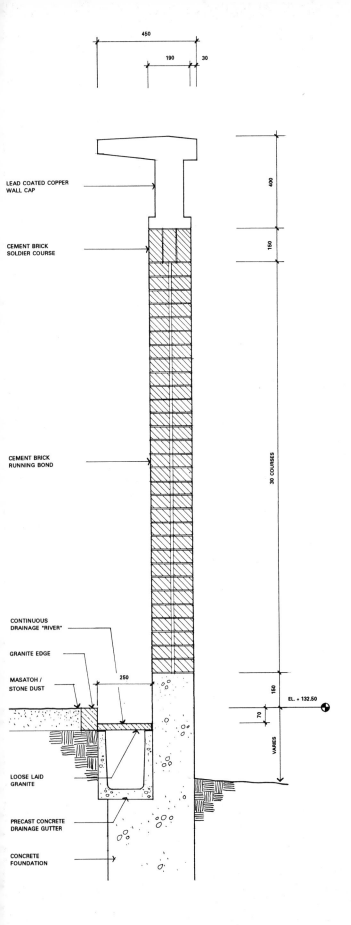

450

190   30

400

150

LEAD COATED COPPER
WALL CAP

CEMENT BRICK
SOLDIER COURSE

CEMENT BRICK
RUNNING BOND

30 COURSES

CONTINUOUS
DRAINAGE "RIVER"

GRANITE EDGE

MASATOH /
STONE DUST

250

150

70

EL. + 132.50

LOOSE LAID
GRANITE

VARIES

PRECAST CONCRETE
DRAINAGE GUTTER

CONCRETE
FOUNDATION

46 Steps at south of site (right) Perimeter wall section detail (above)

47 48 View of exterior stair and entry building (above) Second floor hall (right)

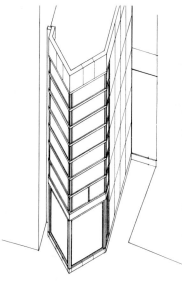

49 50 Secondary stair (left) Night view of secondary stair (top) Secondary stair exterior study (bottom)

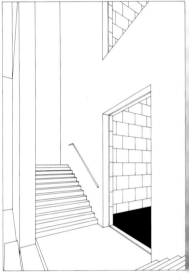

53 54 Central Hall (left and above right) Interior stair perspective (below right)

55 56 Central Hall (above) Ceiling at Central Hall (right)

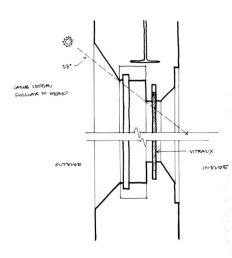

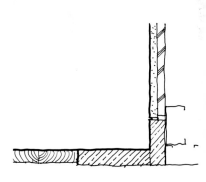

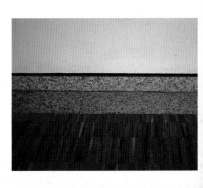

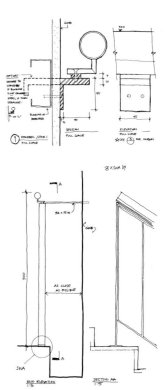

62 63 64 Main stair (left) Secondary stair handrail detail (top) Main stair handrail detail (bottom) Main stair handrail section detail and railing sketch (middle)

65   66   Second floor connecting gallery (above)   Main stair (right)

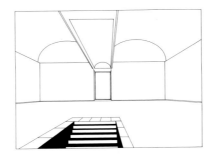

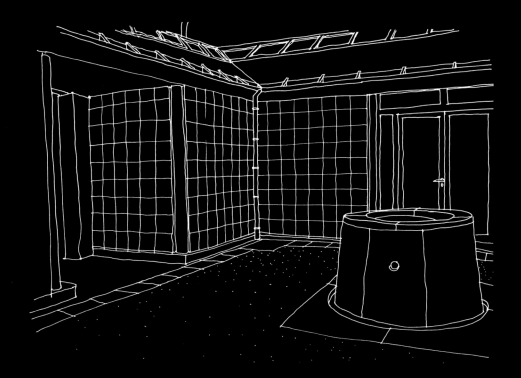

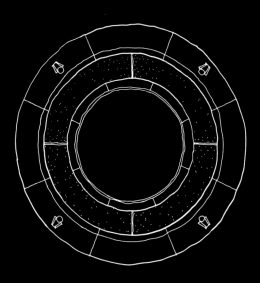

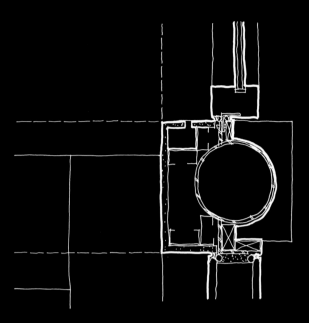

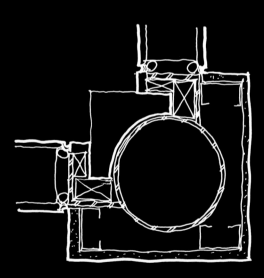

Column detail plans (above) Courtyard perspective study (following page upper left) Plan and elevation of light well (following page below)

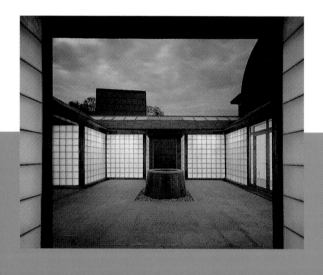

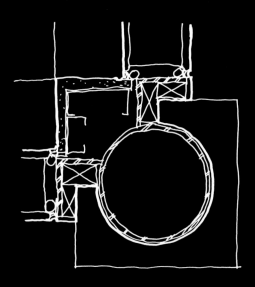

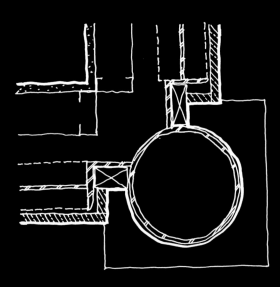

Column detail plans (above) Section at entry to top gallery (previous page above) Light well section detail (previous page below)

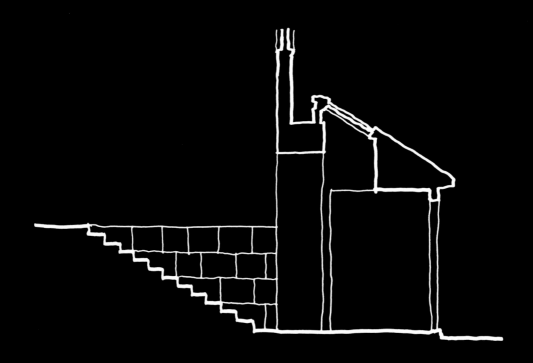

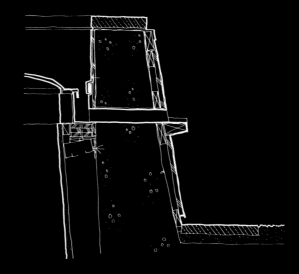

Project Name:	Whanki Museum
Owner:	The Whanki Foundation
Location:	Seoul, Korea
Architect:	Kyu Sung Woo Architect Inc.

488 Green Street
Cambridge, Massachusetts
02139
617-547-0128

Aum, Duck-Moon Award in Architecture, Korean Institute of Architects, 1995
Kim Swoo Geun Award for Cultural Achievement, Kim Swoo Geun Foundation, 1994
Award for Excellence in Architecture, New England Regional Council, American Institute of Architects, 1992
Award for Excellence in Architecture, Boston Society of Architects, 1991

Design Team:	Kyu Sung Woo, principal in charge	Vitraux/Stained Glass:	S.A.R.L. Vitraux Dhonneur
	Steve Lacker, associate		
	Austin Smith, Steve Baker,	General Contractor:	Pull Ham Construction Co. Ltd.
	project architects		1581-13 Seo-Cho-Dong Seo-
	Andrew Wang, Pablo Nistal, Laura Burns,		Cho-Ku
	Dennis Carlberg, Donald Powers,		Seoul, Korea
	Sheryl Kurtz Halberstadt, Sun Young Rieh,		
	Nicholas Isaak, Naomi Neville,	Building Area:	11,470 square feet (Main
	Karen Drozda, Adolfo Perez, project team		building)
			4,600 square feet (Annex)
Associated Architect:	Ilkun Architects & Consulting Engineers	Date of Design:	1988-1992
	Seoul, Korea Kim In-Seok, principal		
	Dyne Architects Seoul, Korea	Date of Completion:	Winter 1993
	Jang Kwang Yeob, Bahng Joon, principals		

Consultants:

	Structural:	Hana Group Architects & Consulting Engineers
	Mechanical:	Bow M.I.E. Consultants
		Cosentini Associates
	Electrical:	Sae Han Engineer Consultants
	Lighting:	Powell Lighting Design
	Landscape:	Michael Van Valkenburgh Associates

Kyu Sung Woo was born in Seoul, Korea in 1941. He received a bachelor of science and master of science degree in arch

engineering at Seoul National University. He came to the United States in 1967, where he studied architecture at Columbia U

and received a master of architecture degree in urban design at Harvard University in 1970. After graduating he worked for J

Sert at Sert, Jackson & Associates (1970-1974). He was a senior urban designer for the Mayor's Office of Midtown Planm

Development, New York, New York (1975). He began his private practice in 1978 and later continued as a principal of Woo and W

In 1990 he formed Kyu Sung Woo Architect, Inc. He has built extensively in both Korea and the United States, including t

Olympic Village in Seoul. Published widely, his work has received national and international recognition. Kyu Sung Woo ha

at the MIT School of Architecture and Planning and the Harvard Graduate School of Design. He is a fellow of the American

of Architects. Recent work includes the Arts of Korea Gallery at the Metropolitan Museum of Art and Harvard University Faculty

Kyu Sung Woo

iginally from Buenos Aires, Oscar Riera Ojeda is an editor and designer who practices in the United States, South America d Europe from his office in Boston. He is vice-director of the Spanish-Argentinian magazine *Casas Internacional,* and is the eator of several series of architectural publications for Rockport Publishers in addition to the *Single Building* series, includ- g *Ten Houses, Contemporary World Architects, Architecture in Detail* and *Art and Architecture.* Other architectural pub- cations include the *New American* series for the Whitney Library of Design, as well as several monographs on the work of nowned architects.

he text was edited by Mark Denton, an architect practicing in Santa Monica, California and New London, Connecticut.

7 78 Night view of entry court (right) Stair to top gallery (following page)

photographic credits

▌ **Timothy Hursley:** 1, 2, 3, 4, 6, 7, 13, 14, 15, 16, 17, 18, 19, 20, 21, 22, 23, 24, 25, 26, 27, 28, 29, 30, 38, 39, 46, 47 48, 49, 50, 51,52, 53, 54, 55, 56, 57, 58, 60, 61, 62, 65, 66, 67, 68, 69, 70, 71, 72, 73, 74, 75, 76, 77, "Stonecloud" photos page 14 ▌ **Lim Chung Eui:** 78 ▌ **Richard Bonarrigo:** 5, 12 ▌ **Chuck Choi:** Arts of Korea Gallery at The Metropolitan Museum of Art, page 12 ▌ **Mick Hales:** Kim House photo, page 14 ▌ **Whanki Museum Archival Department:** Whanki art work, pages 16, 17, Whanki portrait page, 20 ▌ **David Henderson:** Kyu Sung Woo portrait page 128 ▌ **Kyu Sung Woo Architect:** 8, 9, 10, 11, 31, 32, 33, 34, 35, 36, 37, 40, 41, 42, 43, 44, 45, 59, 63, 64